D1557519

ENTITLEMENT ISSUES IN THE DOMESTIC BUDGET

ENTITLEMENT ISSUES IN THE DOMESTIC BUDGET

The Long-Term Agenda

Edited by John C. Weicher

American Enterprise Institute for Public Policy Research
Washington, D. C.

Library of Congress Cataloging in Publication Data
Main entry under title:

Entitlement Issues in the domestic budget.

(AEI symposia ; 85B)
1. Entitlement spending—United States—Congresses. 2. Budget—United States—Congresses. 3. Social Security—United States—Congresses. 4. Medicare—Finance—Congresses. 5. Civil service pensions—United States—Congresses
I. Weicher, John C. II. American Enterprise Institute for Public Policy Research. III. Series.
HJ2052.E57   1985   353.0084   85-20476
ISBN 0-8447-2254-5 (alk. paper)

1 3 5 7 9 10 8 6 4 2

AEI Symposia 85B

Printed in the United States of America

Contents

Contributors

ANNELISE ANDERSON is currently a senior research fellow at the Hoover Institution, Stanford University. She has contributed an article on the federal budget to its recently published book, *To Promote Prosperity: Domestic Policy in the Mid-1980s.* During the first two years of the first Reagan administration, she served as associate director for economics and government, Office of Management and Budget. She holds a Ph.D. in business administration from the Graduate School of Business, Columbia University.

KENNETH W. CLARKSON is professor of economics and director of the Law and Economics Center at the University of Miami. He served as associate director for human resources, veterans, and labor at the Office of Management and Budget during 1982 and 1983. He has been a member of the Advisory Council on Education Statistics of the U.S. Department of Education and a consultant to the President's Task Force on Food Assistance and has written monographs on food stamp and nutrition programs and on unemployment statistics, among many other publications.

MICKEY D. LEVY is senior vice president and chief economist at Fidelity Bank, Philadelphia. He is also a member of the Shadow Open Market Committee and is on the Economic Advisory Committees of the American and Pennsylvania Bankers Associations. Previously, he was an economist at the American Enterprise Institute and the Congressional Budget Office. He is the author of *The Tax Treatment of Social Security.* His recent research has been in monetary and fiscal policies and their interaction, economic forecasting, and financial market behavior.

JACK A. MEYER is a resident fellow in economics and director of the Center for Health Policy Research at AEI. He has served as a consultant with the Organization for Economic Cooperation and Development on the subject of health and aging. He was formerly assistant director of the U.S. Council on Wage and Price Stability. His most recent book is *Passing the Health Care Buck: Who Pays the Hidden Costs?* He has also edited *Incentives vs. Controls in Health Policy: Broadening the Debate.*

JOHN C. WEICHER holds the F. K. Weyerhaeuser Chair in Public Policy Research at AEI. He has served with the President's Commission on Housing and as chief economist at the U.S. Department of Housing and Urban Development. He taught economics at Ohio State University and was director of the housing and financial markets research program at the Urban Institute. Past president of the American Real Estate and Urban Economics Association, he has recently written *Housing: Federal Policies and Programs* and edited *Maintaining the Safety Net: Income Redistribution Programs in the Reagan Administration.*

Foreword

Entitlement programs are the core of the domestic budget of the federal government. They amount to more than two-thirds of federal domestic outlays, excluding interest on the federal debt. Once they are established, entitlement programs are usually discussed within the short-term context of current budget concerns; public policy discussions seldom look further into the future than a year or two, if that far. Structural changes in these programs are therefore seldom given serious attention until problems with the current structure become very large and something must be done to resolve, or at least ameliorate, them.

Yet structural problems can be foreseen, often several years or a decade before they occur. Given the time within which public policy decisions are typically made, informed and dispassionate analyses of the problems should be addressed as far in advance as possible, so that policy makers have available a range of well-thought-out solutions before they are urgently needed.

This volume provides analyses of some fundamental problems in several of the most important entitlement programs: social security, Medicare, civil service retirement, programs for the poor, and others. At the end of President Reagan's first term—and before the first budget of his second term had been prepared—the American Enterprise Institute invited four experts on various categories of the federal domestic budget to discuss the issues that seemed important to them. They chose to concentrate on long-term problems in the major entitlement programs, rather than on the issues then receiving most of the press and public attention. This emphasis may be surprising, considering the great attention given to the federal budget deficit over the past few years. The analysts, however, felt that important issues, with far-reaching consequences, were likely to be ignored in the current budget debate and attempted to redress the balance. We believe that their analyses and recommendations are worth serious attention, even if the problems they address are not yet crises.

WILLIAM J. BAROODY
President
American Enterprise Institute

ix

Introduction

John C. Weicher

The second Reagan administration has begun with the federal budget again at the center of public discussion and with various proposals to restrain its growth being advocated by the president and members of Congress. This continues the pattern established during President Reagan's first term, in which most major policy issues—particularly in the domestic program area—have been addressed within the framework of the federal budget. It seems likely to remain the pattern for the next four years, if not beyond.

Scholars at the American Enterprise Institute have regularly participated in the budget debates. This volume offers a further contribution. During our 1984 Public Policy Week—conducted in December, midway between the president's reelection and his second inauguration—AEI convened a distinguished panel to discuss "The Domestic Budget Agenda: The Next Four Years." The four panelists are all recognized experts on key areas of the domestic budget; between them, they have conducted research, or had administrative responsibility within the federal government, in areas that constitute over 90 percent of the domestic budget.

AEI asked these experts to discuss any aspect of the domestic budget that they wished. At the time, the administration was beginning to formulate the first budget of the president's second term, and press reports indicated that it would propose substantial cuts in domestic spending. The panelists, however, chose to focus their attention on fundamental long-term problems and needed structural reforms in the major entitlement programs, rather than on the short-term possibilities of cutting the budget.

In social security, for example, Mickey Levy of Fidelity Bank stressed the problems created by the present federal income tax treatment of benefits and the unfairness of the spouse benefit, which now provides benefits for working wives lower than those they would receive had they never worked outside the home.

Jack Meyer, director of AEI's Health Policy Studies Center, examined Medicare and Medicaid, noting that they were expensive programs

1

that yet failed to provide adequate coverage in many respects, particularly for those with needs for long-term hospitalization, and for the low-income elderly who are slightly above the poverty line and thus ineligible for Medicaid. Both Dr. Levy and Dr. Meyer noted current projections that these programs are now in good financial condition for at least the next ten years and, while expressing some skepticism about the validity of the projections, urged that attention be given now to basic problems, rather than waiting for the next fiscal crisis.

Annelise Anderson of the Hoover Institution, a former associate director of the Office of Management and Budget, concentrated on civil service pay and retirement. She argued simultaneously that federal workers are overpaid and underpaid; they are supposed to be paid on the same scale as comparable private workers but are frequently assigned to higher grades—and are thus paid more than the private employees doing the same work. This overpayment is combined with an extremely generous retirement system. At the same time, those federal workers whose responsibilities are greatest tend to be paid less than their private sector counterparts.

Kenneth Clarkson of Miami University, also a former associate director of OMB, concentrated on low-income benefit programs. He addressed particularly the long-recognized problem that some beneficiaries are able to combine assistance from many programs into a large total, while others receive little. He also proposed that domestic programs generally should be subjected to a more stringent test of national necessity, including whether they compete with the private sector or can be handled more effectively by state or local governments.

All of the panelists offered detailed suggestions for resolving or at least ameliorating the problems they identified. Dr. Levy recommended taxing benefits in excess of lifetime contributions in a manner similar to the tax treatment of private pensions. Dr. Meyer recommended a restructuring of Medicaid in line with the administration's fiscal year 1984 budget proposal, requiring some cost sharing by beneficiaries for routine services and problems, in conjunction with catastrophic illness protection. Dr. Anderson suggested changes in the retirement benefits formula, notably the cost-of-living adjustment and the earnings base used to calculate retirement income; she also proposed a system of controls for the number of federal workers in different grades, to prevent overpayment. Dr. Clarkson recommended that total benefits received by each individual should be integrated with the income tax system and subject to a graduated tax.

In the months since our panel met, it is fair to say that public policy has not seriously addressed many of the problems raised. The president's budget for fiscal year 1986 did propose some of the Medicare reforms

2

advocated by Dr. Meyer, particularly an increase in the share of supplementary medical insurance premiums paid by beneficiaries. It also advocated a voluntary Medicare voucher that beneficiaries could use to buy private health insurance. Beyond this, however, it proposed to control costs by continuing a freeze on Medicare payments to physicians and other services. Minor changes in low-income programs included Dr. Clarkson's recommendation that Aid to Families with Dependent Children should not be provided to minor single mothers if they move out of their parents' residence, but the budget did not address the more basic problem of coordinating benefits across programs. Nor did it propose fundamental reforms in civil service pay or retirement, recommending instead freezes in the latter and an across-the-board pay cut for federal workers. It did not propose any change in social security at all.

Congress has similarly ignored the basic problems. Issues in the major entitlement programs have been framed in terms of whether to freeze or not to freeze. For example, the Senate voted to defer cost-of-living increases in the retirement programs for the next fiscal year and to hold federal pay constant for a year; the House favored allowing benefits and pay to rise with inflation. They have agreed to an increase in medical insurance premium payments, half the amount proposed by the administration; otherwise, no significant structural reforms were approved in the fiscal year 1986 budget resolution.

One consequence of this failure to act is that the issues raised by our panel remain timely and continue to deserve the attention of policymakers and the public. For this reason, AEI is publishing the proceedings of the discussion, including both the remarks of the panelists and the lively discussion that ensued among members of the audience and the panel. It is perhaps worth noting that the audience, like the panel, was unconstrained in its choice of subject but was also primarily concerned with structural problems in the major entitlement programs. This may suggest that there is more public concern with the problems than is being expressed within the context of the current budget debate.

Social Security: Financing Rising Benefits and Other Issues

Mickey D. Levy

The improved financial outlook for the social security trust funds, reflecting primarily the recent strong economic performance and the cost-saving provisions of the Social Security Amendments of 1983, has been a pleasant change from the persistent threat of insolvency from 1973 to 1983. Recent official reports forecast accumulating balances in social security's Old-Age Survivors Insurance and Disability Insurance (OASI and DI or, combined, OASDI) trust funds during the next several decades and an approximate long-run balance between annual average income and outgo of the combined trust funds (OASDI) if the economy follows a steady-state growth path. Yet one unfortunate consequence of the apparent renewed financial soundness of social security is that the program has become a less pressing issue, despite its many problems. That trust fund revenues have exceeded outgo for two years is insufficient reason to ignore social security's glaring intra- and intergenerational inequities and its potentially large adverse impacts on personal savings and labor supply, nor is it a valid basis for projecting long-run financial soundness. Rather than being complacent, I argue that the unfinished legislative agenda for social security is lengthy and that now is the proper time to take steps toward improving some of the system's flaws. And while I acknowledge the immense financial difficulty facing the Hospital Insurance (HI) trust fund and the absolute need for a broad reform of Medicare, I do not address that program in my remarks.

In fiscal year 1985, expenditures for social security and Medicare will be approximately $258 billion, or 27.7 percent of total federal outlays and 6.5 percent of gross national product (GNP). This compares with 18.7 percent of federal outlays and 3.8 percent of GNP in 1970. Social security outlays are forecast to rise substantially further in inflation-adjusted terms and as a percentage of federal outlays and GNP. Nevertheless, recent public declarations by political candidates have reaffirmed

4

social security as the ultimate "sacred cow" among federal spending programs. In the near term, meaningful debate about reform among elected policy makers seems highly improbable; in the longer run, reform efforts will be constrained by the rising age of the median voter and the associated heightened pressures to maintain scheduled benefit levels. Nevertheless, sooner or later, program modifications will be necessary. Recommendations with the largest probability of passage will likely involve adjustments in the current social security structure that accommodate the short-term concerns of elected policy makers.

A Brief Financial Review

Two years ago when, at the trough of the recession, insolvency of the OASI and DI trust funds was considered imminent, a large long-run actuarial imbalance hovered over the social security landscape like a dark cloud. Threatened by the short-run financing dilemma, the 1983 amendments were enacted. They generated approximately $165 billion in saving between 1983 and 1989 (with most of the savings in the last two years) and provided a long-run average annual savings of 2.08 percent of taxable payroll (over a seventy-five-year projection period). Assuming continued economic expansion, these amendments resolve the short-run financial imbalance of OASI and DI, largely through payroll tax increases, extended coverage, and general fund transfers. Roughly half of the long-run savings were due to reduced benefit growth, a delayed phased-in increase in the retirement age.[1] The 1983 amendments largely ignored the mounting problems facing Medicare. Under current law, Medicare outlays are forecast to rise substantially in real terms and to far exceed scheduled tax rates as a percentage of taxable payroll. The HI trust fund is expected to become insolvent in the early 1990s and fall further into debt thereafter.

Most of the short-run improvement in social security's financial status since late 1982 is attributable to the dramatic turnaround in the economy. Renewed increases in real wages have allowed payroll tax revenue growth to exceed the growth of indexed cash benefits. Also, the 6.5 million increase in employment since year-end 1982 has boosted revenues. Thus, a word of caution should be attached to the healthier financial status of social security: one should not simply project future conditions of the trust funds from the recent sharp improvement. The program's finances are extremely sensitive to economic cycles, and financial planning based on the assumption of uninterrupted economic and real wage growth, as is the practice in the Annual Reports of the Trustees of the Social Security System, is shortsighted.

The long-run financial outlook for social security has improved mainly because of legislated tax increases, benefit cuts (particularly the phased-in increase in the retirement age), and extended coverage of the 1983 amendments. Also, the very strong economic performance since late 1982 makes the economic assumptions underlying the long-run projections seemingly attainable. Yet the experience of the 1970s taught us what can go wrong with the economy. Accordingly, given the sensitivity of payroll taxes and cash benefits to economic and demographic factors, the most prudent assessment is that the system's long-run financial outlook is uncertain. Importantly, the recent change in the way benefits are indexed protects the financial status of the trust funds when real wages decline.[2] The funds, however, remain very sensitive to economic cycles and sharp slowdowns in real wage growth. For example, in the 1984 Annual Report, a one-percentage-point difference in the annual rate of real wage growth is one of the key factors that distinguishes long-run financial solvency (Alternative II-A) from a large long-run actuarial deficit (in Alternative III, the average annual shortfall is 4.12 percent of taxable payroll).

Thus, strictly from the financing angle, an approximate long-run actuarial balance based on steady-stage growth of real GNP and real wages may not be a sufficient financial cushion in light of what may go wrong. During the next several years, combined OASDI trust fund balances will never exceed three months of benefits, and the thinness of this contingency fund makes social security a potentially destabilizing economic factor. For example, an economic downturn would threaten trust fund solvency; higher payroll taxes or benefit cuts to avoid insolvency would further aggravate any weakness in disposable personal income. Social security's long-run financial outlook will also deteriorate in each succeeding year's annual report as the first year of the preceding year's projection (showing approximate balance or a slight surplus) will be replaced by a sizable deficit in the "new" last year of the long-term projections.

This brief review of social security's financial status suggests that there is no need for alarm. Policy makers, however, must be aware that a financial imbalance could reemerge quickly. Because reforms of social security require long periods of implementation, now is the time to develop a long-term strategy.

Problems beyond Financial Solvency

The improved financial status of social security may have several potentially unintended and undesirable consequences for the system's future. Unless a short-run financial crisis is imminent, the program is shuffled immediately to a low-priority status by elected officials. The "calm" following the passage of amendments in 1977 and 1983 is a good example of this pattern. Congress and the administration are always willing to "declare victory" once an immediate threat of insolvency is resolved, despite inherent structural flaws in the system. Thus, the recent improvement generates complacency among policy makers at a time when concern is warranted.

Even when short-term financial crises have occurred, past efforts to avoid insolvency have set a poor precedent for future legislative actions. The threat of insolvency in one trust fund typically has been resolved by transferring funds from another fund and/or reallocating future payroll taxes among funds; a tenuous financial status of the combined funds usually solicits interfund transfers and higher payroll tax revenues. Interfund transfers between social security's cash programs, OASI and DI, is proper, but using funds from these programs to postpone addressing the financial difficulties of the Medicare program is misguided. According to recent projections, in the early 1990s, OASDI trust fund balances will be accumulating, while the HI fund for Medicare will be moving rapidly toward insolvency. An interfund transfer would only evade the real issue: that Medicare as an open-ended entitlement program requires structural reform to slow its rate of outlay growth. Also, in the past, as trust fund balances have accumulated, pressure has mounted to disburse the surpluses, always in the form of liberalized benefits or expanded eligibility, never as payroll tax cuts. Such pressures must be rejected in the future.

Importantly, the way in which social security is evaluated, with primary focus on the trust fund balances and the long-run actuarial (im)balance—the relationship between annual payroll tax revenues and outlays (as a percentage of taxable income)—provides a very limited and, in certain ways, misleading profile of the system's finances. Analogously, an analysis of the federal unified budget would be limited if it considered only budget deficits (surpluses) and the government debt, ignoring the patterns of outlays and taxes and what those patterns may imply for (dis)incentives to work, save, and invest and for economic performance in general, as well as the fairness of their distribution. Social security issues as basic as program intent, equity, adequacy, and affordability are often ignored, or, because of the more popular concerns about financial solvency of the trust funds, attempts to cope with them are misguided. Also, social security's increased outlays as a share of total budget outlays, and its competition for public funds, must be recognized. For example, while recent official social security projections indicate an approximate long-run actuarial balance, social security benefits are scheduled to rise, in real terms and as a percentage of federal budget outlays and GNP. This opens up several important issues: is it necessary (or proper) for real (inflation-adjusted) benefits to rise, even as individuals in future generations become wealthier and are better able to save and plan for retirement? Moreover, is the scheduled increase in benefits affordable?

The debate about the adequacy of social security benefits has usually been incomplete and misinformed, in several ways. For example, the debate overlooks how the income and wealth profiles of the elderly have changed in recent decades. On average, the elderly are much better off than the aged several decades ago. Taking into account taxes, transfers, in-kind benefits, and family size, the elderly now may be as well off economically as the nonaged, and they have proved to be equally capable of protecting their wealth against inflation.[3] In addition, the aged have a continuing propensity to save, contrary to what one would expect from a life-cycle hypothesis. Yet the public perception of the economic status of the elderly has lagged behind actual improvement, greatly influencing policy makers.

Individuals in succeeding generations will become wealthier as the economy expands and real wages rise. In addition, several vehicles for private saving have been enhanced and will provide vastly improved financial support to future retirees. The government now provides a broadened range of financial incentives to save that are becoming increasingly important in retirement planning (for example, IRAs, Keoghs, and 401(k)s, and the like). Moreover, a growing portion of employees are becoming vested in private pensions, and the present value of pension wealth is rising significantly as many recently established pensions "mature." Yet, under the current social security benefit structure, real benefits will rise. Should the concept of benefit "adequacy" consider private sources of saving? The answer is definitely yes, if the goal of social security is to provide financial security to the needy elderly; and probably yes, even if the (implicit) goal of social security is a combination of an insurance and tax-transfer program. There is, however, some concern about the costs of supporting such rising real benefits under uncertain economic conditions, particularly when other demands compete for public funds.

Most social security analysts have provided poor guidance to policy makers on the issue of benefit adequacy by emphasizing primarily the "replacement rate"—the initial year's benefits received by a retiree divided by earnings in the year before retirement—and suggesting that some constant average replacement rate is both adequate and equitable. The measure fails on all counts: it ignores the economic status of the elderly and their other sources of income and wealth; it does not relate benefits to lifetime earnings and payroll tax contributions; it ignores the fact that the vast majority of benefits are exempt from taxation (before the 1983 amendments, all benefits were excluded from taxation) while wages earned in the year before retirement are subject to income and payroll taxes. Moreover, a constant average replacement rate is often misused to imply constant benefits. Despite these many flaws, the replacement rate unfortunately is a very influential criterion for policy makers.

Noticeably absent from the social security debate is the consideration of benefit adequacy within the context of affordability. Certainly, in mechanized steady-state growth models, this issue is not a concern. Scheduled benefits become affordable, and the system becomes actuarially balanced merely by imposing higher payroll taxes. But the issue deserves careful analysis, in terms of simple budget arithmetic and also the economic effects of higher taxes and benefits. In fiscal year 1985, OASDI and Medicare benefits will equal approximately 14 percent of taxable payroll, 27.7 percent of total federal outlays, and 6.5 percent of GNP. In 2005, even before the postwar babyboom children retire, these benefits are forecast to rise to over 15 percent of taxable payroll and absorb a larger portion of federal outlays and GNP. All of the increase is expected to be in Medicare outlays. As the contest for public funds intensifies (for example, through the 1980s outlays for defense and interest also are forecast to absorb larger portions of total outlays and GNP), is it reasonable that scheduled rises in social security benefits remain sacrosanct? The potential conflict between competing demands on taxpayers will not disappear: twenty-five years later, in 2030, if total benefits rise to 23.7 percent of taxable payroll, as projected in the 1984 trustees' "intermediate path," they will absorb 9.4 percent of GNP and 40 percent of federal outlays, if total federal outlays remain at their current proportion of GNP.

Beyond simple arithmetic, the issue of economic viability concerns the potential adverse impacts of rising payroll taxes and social security benefits on work effort, saving, and economic growth generally. Unfortunately, the economic consequences of higher payroll taxes and social security benefits are uncertain. Economists have reached no consensus on the impacts of social security on labor supply or private saving. Regarding the issue of labor supply, the trend toward early retirement has continued, as evidenced by the dramatic decline in the labor force participation rates of men and women. Social security's indexed and largely tax-exempt benefits and its benefit structure and retirement test have contributed to the trend toward early retirement, although we do not know by how much. And while the impact of social security on saving perhaps is more difficult to quantify, the long-run economic stakes are high: if social security does depress private saving, as some analysts contend, the adverse economic consequences are potentially immense. Given these unknown and potentially large harmful effects, prudent policy making should follow a cautious approach, particularly in light of the mounting conflict between rising benefits and program affordability.

More readily apparent than the program's economic effects, some of the inequitable characteristics of social security are sizable in magnitude. Perhaps the largest source of intragenerational unfairness among social security participants is the social security spouse benefit, which effectively discriminates against working women and single workers. Typically, the benefits of working wives based on their own work histories are less than the amount provided by spouse benefits had they never worked; that is, the effective rate of return on their payroll taxes is zero. That social security's treatment of women has not evolved over the past four decades with the dramatic change in the role of women in the labor force is inexcusable.[4] Several of social security's other intragenerational inequities continued to exist, despite provisions of the 1983 amendments that addressed them. Windfall benefits accrue to the sizable number of government employees that now receive or will be eligible in the future to receive both government pensions and social security benefits. While the 1983 amendments extended social security coverage to new government employees, the overly long implementation period will allow the inequity to remain and the unnecessary costs generated by the pre-existing eligibility structure to continue to mount during the next several decades. This is a clear case in which policy makers have buckled under heavy political lobbying by a minority that directly benefits from a glaring inequity. Also, the largest portion of social security benefits are tax exempt (the 1983 amendments required that 50 percent of benefits be added to the taxable incomes of recipients if their adjusted gross income, including social security benefits and income from tax-exempt debt securities, exceeds $25,000 for individuals and $32,000 for married taxpayers filing jointly). Therefore, the after-tax value of each dollar of social security benefit in general rises with income, providing a financial advantage to recipients with other sources of income but not to low-income recipients. This is another example of how social security has failed to adjust to changing events: in this case, the gradual rise and increasing importance of marginal tax rates since benefits were first paid. Another type of inequity between social security recipients whose benefits are indexed to inflation and workers whose real (after-tax) wages may decline was partially eliminated by a provision in the 1983 amendments, which changed the indexation of benefits to the lower of the increase of wages or prices, under certain conditions. My concern is twofold: that using a trust fund ratio as a threshold for determining an equity-related issue is highly arbitrary and that elected officials always seem more than eager to provide the cost-of-living adjustment (COLA). Will the new COLA provision be circumvented when it is time to implement it?

A major intergenerational inequity is also typically overlooked and seemingly inconsistent with social security's fundamental function of forced saving and intergenerational transfers: rates of return on payroll tax contributions will be substantially lower for future generations of retirees than for current retirees or older workers soon to retire. The unequal rate of return across generations is not a particularly solid basis for a program that ultimately must rely on intergenerational cooperation.

Suggestions for Program Adjustments

The major stumbling block to eliminating some of these inequities is the ingrained notion among social security policy makers that achieving equity implies, or is constrained by, the precept of "holding everyone harmless" (at least as well off as before). That is, "improving equity" typically has involved providing more benefits to one group, rather than reducing them for another, which obviously has implied higher overall benefits and program costs. Such a practice evolved during the decades when the system was maturing, when program benefits and costs were well below current levels, and when the elderly were substantially poorer than today. Certainly, the benefit cuts in the 1977 and 1983 amendments deviated from this general trend, but they were relatively minor and, to date, are the exception rather than the rule. The recent political rhetoric about social security has seemingly lost sight of the system's purpose, the changing economic profile of the population cohort it is supposed to serve, the tax burden it puts on workers (particularly "middle income" workers not eligible for the earned income credit), and the overall federal budget context in which it operates. (A provision of the 1983 amendments removes social security from the unified budget in 1992.)

Yet the ingrained social contract implied by the social security bene-fit structure may not be economically viable. Economic and budgetary rationality must be substituted for the tiresome and fruitless debate about whether social security is an insurance program or a tax-transfer program. The aged population is no longer homogeneous economically: similar to the nonaged population, its wide distribution of income and wealth suggests strongly that social security's current structure as a non-means-tested entitlement is an inefficient and costly method of address-ing the financial needs of the poor elderly. In an attempt to meet the needs of the poor elderly, is it necessary or desirable to provide income support to the upper-income aged? I recommend that the guiding prin-ciple of holding everyone harmless be replaced by the more financially responsible notion of striking a balance between what is fair to the wide range of beneficiaries and what is fair to the wide range of workers who must bear the financial burden of the benefits. Such a balance requires recognizing that some recipients are more financially able to absorb reductions in net benefits and that the economic viability of financing benefits is determined in part by the impact of higher payroll taxes and benefits on decisions to work, retire, and save.

Given the political sensitivity of the social security issue, any program modifications almost necessarily involve altering the current structure of taxes or benefits, despite the appeal to some analysts of radical reform. Within this context, however, much can be accomplished. Although many of the issues mentioned below are well known to social security analysts, they are worth repeating because, sooner or later, program changes will be necessary.

The system should be modified wherever feasible to neutralize its impact on workers' decisions to retire. This would involve immediate elimination of the retirement test (currently, benefits are reduced $1 for every $2 in annual wages in excess of a base amount; the 1983 amendments lessened the effect to $1 for every $3 in wages, but not until 1990); faster implementation of the change in the benefit structure that provides actuarially equivalent benefits, regardless of when a worker retires; and a further modification of the benefit COLA by eliminating the thresholds for triggering the lower of the increase in wages or prices provision. Also, social security's treatment of women should be altered by replacing the spouse benefit provision with an earnings-sharing arrangement whereby spouses would divide evenly covered household earnings, so that each spouse's benefits would be based on his or her own earnings base. This would eliminate most of the inequities created by the changing role of women in the labor force and changing family structure.

These alterations could be implemented so that total benefits would not be affected. Independent of their net impact on benefits, these changes would make long strides toward equity and economic efficiency. Yet it must be emphasized that improvement does not imply helping some while making nobody worse off.

Another much-needed change involves taxing benefits that exceed lifetime contributions, analogous to the tax treatment of private pensions. The advantages of such a change over the watered-down tax provisions in the 1983 amendments are surprising.[5] It would broaden the personal income tax base and tax income more evenly, regardless of source, and it would eliminate the financial advantage now provided to recipients with income from other sources without having any impact on poorer recipients that rely heavily on benefits as their primary source of income. In this regard, by providing a larger portion of net benefits to lower-income recipients, it would be much more equitable than lowering the benefit COLA, which reduces benefits of all recipients, even the poorest. On a household basis, taxing benefits that exceed contributions would reduce the extent to which social security discriminates against single workers and married working women. This tax treatment also would reduce significantly the disparity of net rates of return on lifetime payroll taxes received by different generations of retirees. Current retirees receiving very high rates of return on lifetime contributions would include a large portion of benefits in taxable income, while future generations of retirees that will receive much lower rates of return will have substantially lower portions of benefits that exceed contributions and are subject to taxation. Taxing benefits that exceed contributions also would discourage early retirement. On the tax treatment issue, I would be willing to funnel a portion of the increased tax revenues back into the system to be used to further enhance the benefits for the truly needy elderly, but an even portion should be used to reduce scheduled payroll taxes.

Another potential area for reform involves changing the basic benefit structure and the calculation of the Primary Insurance Amount in a way that would slow the scheduled rise in the growth of real benefits. The issue of how average indexed monthly earnings should be calculated and how the benefit rates should be structured affects the desired level of future benefits, and it also involves complex topics of intra- and intergenerational equity.[6] I believe such issues deserve close attention, despite the limited appetite of policy makers to consider them.

Concluding Remarks

This brief review of selected social security issues should leave one unsettled and frustrated. Clearly, the system's original intent of providing financial support for the needy elderly is vital to the role of government. Yet the system has been extended well beyond its original intent, and it has not been modified to accommodate a dramatically changing economic environment: the improved economic status of many aged, the rising participation of women in the labor force, the changing demographics, the higher federal spending and taxes, and the sharpened competition for public funds and the associated federal budget dilemma. It seems obvious that social security should be adjusted to provide more efficient—and perhaps more generous—support to the needy elderly. But this requires acknowledging that the current system is not the most cost-effective method of meeting the needs of the increasingly heterogeneous economic nature of the aged cohort. Unfortunately, most social security analysts have narrowly defined the issue solely in terms of financial solvency and otherwise have provided an erroneous framework for analyzing the system. Most important, policy makers have not faced the basic issues. As an intergenerational system, social security requires a long-run perspective that is seemingly beyond the time horizon of most elected officials. Current political priorities suggest that social security will not reemerge as a burning policy issue until the next financial crisis and, even then, many basic and important issues will be overshadowed by expedient efforts to ensure short-run financial solvency. A different outcome would require a shift in political incentives that now face elected officials.

Notes

1. For a brief review of the 1983 amendments, see Mickey D. Levy, "Social Security: Vast Improvement but Major Problems Remain," *AEI Economist*, April 1983.

2. A provision of the 1983 amendments indexes benefits to the lower of the annual increase in wages or prices if the combined trust fund "ratio" (balances divided by annual outgo) of OASI and DI is below 15 percent, with a catch-up in ensuing years when real wages rise and the trust fund ratio exceeds 32 percent.

3. Henry Aaron, "Summary of Remarks by Henry Aaron to the National Commission on Social Security Reform," August 20, 1982; Michael Hurd and John B. Shoven, "Real Income and Wealth of the Elderly," *American Economic Review,* May 1982, pp. 314–18 and "The Economic Status of the Elderly: 1969–1979," Prepared for an NBER Conference on Research in Income and Wealth, December 8–9, 1983; Barbara Boyle Torrey, "Discussion of Income Transfers and the Economic Status of the Elderly," Office of Management and Budget, unpublished manuscript, and "Estimating After Tax Money Income Distributions," *Current Population Reports* Number 126, U.S. Department of Commerce, Bureau of the Census, 1983.

4. It is also ironic that all politicians urge private employers to provide competitive (or equal or comparable) pay for women, without recognizing that the government, through social security's treatment of women, is a major source of inequitable compensation between men and women.

5. These issues are spelled out in detail in Mickey D. Levy, *The Tax Treatment of Social Security* (Washington, D.C.: American Enterprise Institute, 1980).

6. See Dean Leimer, Ronald Hoffman, and Alan Freiden, "A Framework for Analyzing the Equity of the Social Security Benefit Structure," U.S. Department of Health, Education, and Welfare *Studies in Income Distribution,* January 1978.

Major Issues in Medicare

Jack A. Meyer

I will begin with a quotation from Winston Churchill taken from a speech in Glasgow, Scotland, on October 11, 1906. These words will help set my theme and suggest that all good ideas are not brand new. On that occasion Churchill said:

> The state must increasingly concern itself with the care of the sick and the aged, and above all, the children. I look forward to the universal establishment of minimum standards of life and labor, but I do not want to see impaired the vigor of competition. We want to draw a line below which we will not allow persons to live and labor, yet above which they may compete with all their strength. We want to have free competition upwards. We do not want to pull down the structures of science and civilization, but rather, to spread a net over the abyss.

Why are Americans exposed, as they are, to very high health care outlays in their old age, at the same time that the government program that is supposed to take care of those outlays—Medicare—is going broke? If a government program is running out of money, we would imagine it to be covering most everything. Yet, our government program for the elderly covers only about 45 percent of their health care expenditures. What Medicare covers, it covers very completely and very generously, while at the same time it does not cover some health expenses at all.

One type of expenditure that Medicare does not cover, with some limited exceptions, is long-term care for the elderly. To be sure, Medicare does pay for up to 100 days in a skilled nursing facility, but many nursing homes do not qualify, and the very expensive stays run well beyond 100 days.

Essentially, we provide no help in this country for middle-class people with chronic illness who need long-term care. If a person becomes completely destitute through spending his own assets, if he can go through

15

the waiting list procedure, and in some cases, if he offers a lump-sum payment "under-the-table" or promises to pay private sector rates even though he is a public sector patient, then he may get some government help in a nursing home. If he does not meet these terms, though, he gets nothing. Our public assistance is an all-or-nothing situation.

One of the major problems that must be addressed is this imbalance in Medicare, a program that covers up to 80 percent of a doctor bill for a routine office visit and at the same time does not cover any costs for some types of very expensive chronic care.

I can be more optimistic about a second problem underlying the Medicare system—the inefficiency in the payment system. We are now starting to change the "gravy train" payment system that has characterized Medicare over the years. This system did not drop down from the heavens: it was picked up and copied exactly as we found it in the private sector in 1965. The medical establishment and the private sector dropped their vigorous opposition to Medicare when the government agreed to pay for medical expenses for the elderly in the same way that Blue Cross paid in the private sector. In other words, the government agreed to reimburse whatever expenses were incurred. The government did not agree to reimburse 100 percent of costs, but the costs of whatever items were deemed "allowable" were reimbursed to all providers of health care alike, irrespective of their costs. Thus, if 90 percent of full costs were made allowable, a provider with double the community wide average billing would still be reimbursed for 90 percent of his costs. Thus, there was no real pressure on a doctor or hospital whose costs were out of line. Furthermore, it is difficult for a cost-conscious doctor or hospital to compete effectively for patients when the profligate provider can simply pass through his excessive costs.

With Churchill's words, which I cited earlier, in mind, let us try to eliminate such inefficiencies in the system and instill more competition into it, at the same time realizing that we must, in his words, "spread a net over the abyss," protecting those not fortunate enough to have resources to compete in the medical service market.

The Outlook for Medicare

With regard to the outlook for the Medicare trust fund, I have some good news and some bad news. One of my distinguished colleagues, Ben Wattenberg, has a new book out, called *The Good News Is the Bad News Is Wrong*. I want to argue that proposition in health care. I also want to argue the opposite proposition, however, that the bad news is the good news is wrong.

The way out of this paradox is the typical economist's retreat: short run versus long run. In the short run, arbitrarily defined as about ten years, the situation is much better than it seems. In the long run, though, things are much more serious than many people believe.

First, the good news: a dramatic slowing in the rate of increase in Medicare spending has occurred in the past year or so. We are not sure why it has been so dramatic; we have only some clues. Nevertheless, as a result of the slowing in the rate of increase, the surplus in the Hospital Insurance (HI) trust fund, which pays for the hospital component of Medicare, is actually projected by the Congressional Budget Office to grow for the next several years. The CBO forecasts a positive and growing fund balance. Indeed, CBO projects the fund to have a balance of about $20 billion in 1985, to rise steadily to about $50 billion near the end of the 1980s, and then to taper off and edge downward, reaching a state of depletion around 1994. As of late 1984, CBO predicts a deficit in 1995 in the HI trust fund of $56 billion.

In illustration of how good that news is, just a few months ago the CBO projected that the fund would run out of money not in 1994, but in 1989, and that there would be a deficit of some $300 billion instead of $56 billion in the mid-1990s.

These differences indicate how volatile the estimates are. We must be careful before we rely too heavily on the improved forecast: the predictions went from bad to good very quickly and could also go from good to bad very quickly if there is a recession or a resurgence of inflation. About 6 million jobs were created in the last several years, a development that helped all of the government trust funds. The rate of inflation, and therefore the cost of labor and fuel, has slowed considerably, benefiting hospitals. We cannot tell, though, how long we will be blessed with those favorable trends.

Other factors contributing to a bright short-term picture for the trust fund include tax increases earmarked for the HI fund scheduled in 1985 and 1986; they are small, but in this area, everything counts. The payroll tax rate for Medicare went from 1.3 percent for both employees and employers in 1984 to 1.35 percent in 1985 and will rise to 1.45 percent in 1986. Those increases will bring revenues into the fund. In addition, the loan that the HI fund gave the old-age fund (OASI) in the dangerous days before social security was "fixed up," so to speak, is due to be repaid, providing about $12 billion for the HI fund. There is, then, a lot of good news.

Although I am optimistic, these trust fund estimates are extremely volatile. I noticed in the CBO report, for example, that a change of one percentage point per year in its estimate of Medicare outlay increases caused a change in the trust fund deficit in 1994 of about $80 billion, on a cumulative basis. These outlays, which have been increasing at "only" 11 percent per year recently, are the same outlays that averaged an increase of 17.7 percent per year between 1970 and 1982. If health care expenditure increases were to go up to 12 percent instead of 11 percent per year, however, and that difference were projected through 1995, it would spell a difference of $80 billion in added deficits. We cannot be smug.

By the same token, if we continue this recent slowdown in outlays, the situation may be even better than is now contemplated.

Using the Window of Opportunity

In my view, we now have a five- to ten-year window of opportunity to set Medicare on a sound course. I suggest that we use this window for two purposes in this near-term period of plenty and offer some longer-term recommendations for the lean years ahead.

First, we should use the breathing spell to plan for needed long-term changes. Second, we should take some specific steps that will set the stage for a more equitable and efficient long-term direction. What are these specifically?

First, we should redesign Medicare benefits to make coverage more fair. Not only are there inequities in that Medicare covers some health services generously and others insufficiently, but also, even for what Medicare does cover—such as hospitalization—it has a bizarre benefit structure that is hard to reconcile with basic insurance principles. Medicare patients pay for the first day in the hospital but do not pay at all from the second to the fifty-ninth day. Then, at the sixtieth day, the government begins further cost sharing. The Medicare recipient must pay about one-fourth of the daily bill after sixty days. In a $400-a-night hospital, that is $100 a night. After ninety days, cost sharing goes up again. This makes no sense to me. Of course, only a small percentage of people fall into this category, but they fall off a financial cliff, and so do their families.

The Reagan administration should resubmit its prudent 1983 proposal to redesign Medicare benefits. This would make the program more of a catastrophic illness protection package by ensuring that after people have spent a certain proportion of their resources on health care, they are through spending and will not become bankrupt. So that Medicare can pay for catastrophic care, people must pay a larger amount for short-stay or routine costs out-of-pocket. For example, patients could pay 5 percent of the hospital bill for the duration of short-term stays or a little more for a checkup at the doctor's office.

I suggest two changes in the administration's prior proposal to serve these goals. First, we should shield the low-income elderly from this "front-end" cost sharing. They are already paying quite a bit, as a proportion of their incomes. If we ask someone for 5 or 10 percent of a hospital bill, we do not want to ask this of an elderly widow just barely above the poverty line, or just barely above the line where Medicaid picks up the cost sharing. In the physician part of the Medicare program, patients pay 20 percent of the portion of the bill from the doctor that Medicare treats as allowable. If the doctor does not voluntarily "accept assignment" of the Medicare claim, the patient may also be billed by the doctor for an amount over what Medicare allows. Beneficiaries also pay a premium of about $15 a month for their physician coverage. These out-of-pocket expenses can be substantial for lower-income senior citizens, while more well-to-do elderly people can more easily afford them. We should begin now to bring these charges more into line with household resources.

I would also add one other change to the Reagan proposal: I would make it "budget neutral" in the short run. I would not use this program change as a revenue raiser for two reasons. First, we do not need the revenue right now in Medicare, for reasons I have explained; second, it would explain to the elderly that these charges are not a takeaway. Although we may have to limit the size of some benefits later on for the well-to-do, right now we are conducting a "good-government" program, a fairness program, if you will. We are rearranging benefits within the elderly group, not to save money for the Treasury, but to distribute whatever money we have more equitably. In fact, these types of changes are incorporated in legislation introduced into the last Congress by Senator Dave Durenberger.

A second step in the short run would be to move from the complex, yet incomplete, new prospective payment system we have, called DRGs, to a more streamlined and more fully prepaid Medicare payment system. I think the new payment system, which divides procedures and diagnoses into 467 groups and pays a fixed amount per diagnosis, introduces some better incentives into the system. It is a step in the right direction. I also think it is incredibly complicated and destined to become more so. Furthermore, it is incomplete. It sets a price once a patient enters a hospital, rather than setting a price for total care, including admissions.

We now hear talk of a new, unrelated DRG system for nursing homes and another one for doctor bills. This approach might degenerate into a complex and variegated set of price controls, which is the last thing we need. We have had one set of price controls after another in this industry that have been, in my view, abysmal failures. We do not want to add another layer of rigid regulations.

We are at a crossroads with regard to Medicare's DRG policy. We could lead it down a sensible path or we could allow it to be diverted onto a path toward complex controls. I am urging that we use DRGs as a steppingstone to a more efficient system where the government does what it does best—pays an overt subsidy to those in need—and allow the industry to decide how to divide up that subsidy among health care services. The government should not attempt to do what it does worst—try to figure out the right price of a hip replacement, of a hysterectomy, or of a complicated gall bladder operation versus an uncomplicated one. Government just is not very good at that.

Third, I think we should breathe life into and broaden the new, sensible HMO payment system passed by Congress and just implemented by the administration. It has taken a long time to get this on the books at all, much less implemented. Essentially, the new approach allows producers of efficient health plans to share in some of the savings and pass them along to the beneficiaries who join an HMO instead of having government take the savings away. Also, patients no longer have to lay out monthly payments in advance and await government reimbursement. That is the beginning of competition in this segment of the health care industry, and this first step should be lengthened. This can be done by relaxing some of the narrow restrictions that limit the participation in the competition. For example, the new regulations prohibit both cash rebates to patients by HMOs and reinvestment of profits into such areas as recruitment of highly skilled physicians or the purchase of new technology. The savings must now go into expanded coverage. Such restrictions may hurt newer HMOs that need added flexibility to compete for Medicare patients. Such limitations could be relaxed gradually while the government continues to exercise vigilance. The current HMO payment plan could be converted into a real multiple-choice payment system, where a wider variety of efficient health plans can reap the savings. And that, in the long run, is the way to generate savings.

A Gap in the Safety Net

I now want to turn from the Medicare program, with its generous but incomplete coverage for the elderly, to discuss a different kind of gap in the Medicaid program for the nonelderly poor and to suggest how that gap should be closed. I would begin on a small scale the job of providing government assistance for health care to the uncovered poor. Half the poor in this country are outside the health care safety net, up from about one-third a decade ago. I find it unconscionable to be unwilling to alter Medicare benefits for the relatively wealthy elderly and not to touch the federal tax subsidies related to health care (which flow mainly to middle- and upper-income people) at the same time that we are slashing the Medicaid rolls.

Over 400,000 people lost welfare benefits in the past few years, and most of those people lost Medicaid as well, as a result. These are often working poor people whose jobs do not provide health insurance and are thereby left out in the cold. Also excluded are single people without dependent children in the household.

I would like to see the start of a small-scale, federal-state block-grant program providing at least catastrophic illness assistance for this group. It is a national problem, the solution to which should begin in Washington. But that does not mean it has to end in Washington.

Recommendations

Let me conclude with a few suggestions for the long term. First, we know that age-dependency ratios will be going up. We know that technology is exploding. Frankly, I think that the payment system reforms I outlined, or indeed those more regulatory proposals that I do not favor, will not be able to offset the tremendous increase in spending coming from these sources. I do believe, therefore, that we will ultimately face a crisis in Medicare, as in the health care system generally, in the long run if we fail to take steps that go beyond payment system reform. This notion is predicated on my belief that there is not as much pure waste in the health system as many people believe, even though there are a lot of high-cost/low-benefit procedures that are very hard to cut because people want them.

Let me list a few suggestions for reform. First, we should ultimately move from a budget-neutral benefit redesign, which I outlined for the short run, to resource-related benefit changes that are not neutral, but indeed, decrease net dollar outflows from the HI trust fund. The goal here is to provide health insurance protection for the elderly, with benefits related to income and assets and not limited to acute care. In order to build catastrophic illness protection for both acute and long-term care into our public sector safety net, we will have to introduce more cost-sharing for routine care for those who can afford it.

In short, I would broaden benefits, but raise the front-end contribution that people make, varying that contribution with their ability to pay. Note that this is not means testing, in the sense that this term is normally used. No one would be excluded from Medicare on the basis of his or her means. Everyone over a certain age would be eligible for Medicare, but the depth of the subsidy would vary with his or her means. We could achieve these benefit changes in a way that brings more money into the system.

Second, I would repair the gaping hole in the health care safety net. We need to help people more with health care if they need it, regardless of age, and help them less, regardless of age, if they are better off. I look forward, therefore, to two kinds of repairs in the safety net: moving into a fairer system of long-term care and providing some coverage for low-income people with acute care needs that are not covered today.

Of course, we have got to finance that coverage. I am not advocating deficit financing. We must end these inequities, however, whereby some people are in government-paid nursing homes while others, equally poor, are not; and whereby some people receive government-paid hospital care, while others, equally poor, do not.

There are two essential ways to set up a more equitable system. I have already outlined the first, which involves having the more well-to-do elderly contribute a little more, but I do think it would be fair to limit the changes to that. Therefore, I suggest the possibility of raising taxes in the future to meet a portion of the expected shortfall in the HI trust fund. We do not have to take this step now, but in the future a fair solution to the shortfall could involve both benefit restructuring and tax changes. We can debate the type of increased tax. I favor higher taxes on alcohol and tobacco and other excise taxes, along with continued reliance on the payroll tax, but I will not dwell here on the fairness and efficiency of different types of taxes.

In the long run we need to share the burden of strengthening Medicare between tomorrow's elderly and tomorrow's working people. We cannot push it all on tomorrow's elderly, because that is unfair. Neither should we just raise taxes to cover all of these benefits. I propose rearranging benefits, not just raising taxes. Even if we rearrange benefits in a fair way, though, we may still eventually face the need to bring more revenue into the Medicare system. In closing, I reiterate my two suggestions: make Medicare actuarially sound in the long run, and make it fair.

Civil Service Pay and Retirement

Annelise Graebner Anderson

It should be no secret that retirement and health expenditures are major challenges in controlling the federal budget. In 1985 federal expenditures for major retirement and health programs (excluding research) will be $354.2 billion of a total $925.5 billion budget (see table 1). If we add national defense and interest on the debt held by the public, we get $742.3 billion.

The nature of the problem presented by retirement and health expenditures is entirely different from that presented by either national defense or interest on the public debt. Interest on the public debt is not directly controllable by any action of the Congress or the president but is entirely a function of prior and current spending and financing decisions, and current interest rates. By contrast, national defense outlays are highly controllable, not only because national defense expenditures are, on the whole, not entitlements, but also because the Congress rarely decides to spend more for national defense than the president requests— in fact, usually less. Thus the national defense budget may be large, but it is not out of control.

Retirement and health expenditures are quite another matter. Most of the funds go to the retired or elderly and are generally not based on need but are rather entitlements paid, on the whole, without regard to income or wealth. The long-run problem the country faces is demographic: the *number* of retired people will increase, and the ratio of retired people to employed people who have to pay the taxes to fund these programs will increase—from 30 Old-Age Survivors Insurance and Disability Insurance beneficiaries per 100 workers in 1985 to 37 in the year 2015 and 50 in the year 2035.[1]

The long-range nature of these problems suggests that we try to overcome the short-range horizon of elected officials and address the long-term problems created not by the current budget crisis, but by the long-run demographic crisis. We should not be too concerned if the effect on the budget is not immediate; the financial markets will give some credit for solving the long-run problem.

TABLE 1
1985 FEDERAL OUTLAYS (PRESIDENT'S BUDGET)

	Billions of Dollars	Percentage of GNP
Retirement		
Social security and railroad retirement	194.7	
Civil service retirement	23.0	
Military retired pay	17.3	
Veterans' service connected compensation	10.3	
Total, major retirement programs	245.3	6.3
Health		
Medicare	75.7	
Medicaid	22.1	
Veterans' medical care	11.1	
Total, major health programs	108.9	2.8
National defense	272.0	7.0
Interest	116.1	3.0
Total, retirement, health, national defense, and interest	742.3	19.1
Total, federal outlays	925.5	23.8

SOURCE: President's 1985 Budget (Washington, D.C.: Government Printing Office, 1984); "Payments for Individuals" and "Federal Government Finances" (Washington, D.C.: Office of Management and Budget).

Civil Service Retirement System

Social security and health are being addressed by others. My concern here will be another major retirement program, namely, civil service retirement. Civil service retirement is subject to its own demographic characteristics: the number of retirees has increased dramatically in recent years owing to the large number of civilians on the federal payroll during and immediately following World War II. Thus, there were 1.8 million annuitants receiving benefits by 1982, a number now increasing at an average rate of less than 2 percent per year. Expenditures will increase more rapidly, however, because of the benefit characteristics of the system.

Characteristics of Civil Service Retirement. Civil service retirement expenditures are not only high and rising, but the system itself has major undesirable characteristics:

1. It is far more costly to the employer (taxpayers) than the combination of social security and a private pension plan, about 28 percent of payroll rather than 15 percent. (The assumptions on which different estimates are made vary; all show a similar order of magnitude difference. This one is based on Office of Personnel Management [OPM] studies reported by Robert W. Hartman.[2])

2. The system encourages early retirement. Full benefits are paid at age fifty-five for those with thirty years of service, at age sixty for those with twenty years of service, and at age sixty-two for those with five years of service. The benefit received increases with each year of service to a maximum of 80 percent of the salary base.

3. The salary base for benefits is the average of the employee's three highest-earnings years rather than the longer averaging periods characteristic of social security (where earnings are indexed), private pension plans, and the Civil Service Retirement System (CSRS) itself when established, which was ten years. This usually results in a higher replacement-of-final-income ratio (thus contributing to the costliness of the system) and encourages "gaming," for example, staying on the job a few more years if Congress recently raised pay.

4. Unlike most private pensions but like social security, benefits are indexed to the consumer price index. Because this index at times has increased faster than federal pay (and because benefits were, for a time, increased at a rate higher than the CPI), some federal retirees receive more than their counterparts who stayed on the job.

5. Unlike many private pension funds, civil service retirement is not integrated with social security (except for those first taking federal employment after January 1, 1984). As of 1975, many civil service retirees (about 40 percent) also received social security and another 29 percent had qualified but were not yet receiving it.

6. The system is designed to encourage people to stay on until eligible for full retirement, and then leave.

The solution to these problems is not especially complicated: one could increase the retirement age (or reduce the pension actuarially for retirement before sixty-five); base the pension on the highest five, ten, or even fifteen years of average earnings; index pensions by the lower of the CPI or a wage index, either for federal workers or for the U.S. working population as a whole; make the benefit formula less rich, possibly in conjunction with indexation of earnings (the replacement rate is now 56.25 percent of salary for thirty years of service); and reduce the civil service pension by some portion of social security benefits received. Two simultaneous criteria should be considered in evaluating the package of changes: providing a replacement ratio more consistent

25

with the private sector and reducing the long-run normal cost. Whatever combination of options might be chosen, they should be phased in except for the cost-of-living adjustment (COLA) provisions. If changes such as a later retirement age are phased in gradually, there will be little budgetary effect except for the COLA provisions for a decade or so. Nevertheless, the ultimate savings should be substantial. The only other option, which should be considered if reform cannot be achieved, is larger contributions from employees.

Obstacles to Reform. The problem with achieving a more reasonable civil service retirement system is that pension benefits cannot be considered in a vacuum: they are part of the total compensation package received by federal employees. The other major portion is pay. My view is that the federal compensation package should be adequate to recruit and retain federal employees competent to do the work they are expected to do in the most cost-effective manner possible. The view that the more incompetent they are, the less damage they will do, must, I think, be rejected. In such critical areas as keeping track of individual earnings records for social security entitlements, controlling air traffic, prosecuting violators of federal law, controlling fraud and abuse in federal grant programs, and providing civilian support to military functions— and many others—the country would be ill served by incompetence.

Finally, the federal civilian labor force provides the president and his appointees with institutional memory—knowledge of programs, data management, and analysis—that they need to run the government and institute the changes the voters have elected them to undertake. Only with competent civilian—and military—professionals is it possible to have effective civilian leadership of the military and leadership of the nondefense agencies that comes from outside the bureaucracy of the civil service itself. Pay and retirement benefits should therefore be considered simultaneously.

Federal Pay

The current policy of the Congress for civil service pay is comparability with the private sector. To this end, the Bureau of Labor Statistics does annual comparability surveys and has found since 1976 that federal employees are, on the whole, underpaid, given the way the comparisons are made. The only way for an employer to know if in fact he is overpaying or underpaying, however, is to look at the waiting lines: how many people are beating down the door for a chance to take available jobs? The queue depends, of course, on the total compensation package, in which phrase I include not only pay and retirement, health and disability benefits, but also job security, working conditions, flexibility about transfers and the like, and opportunities for advancement.

What, then, of federal pay, a budget category that costs the federal government $64 billion a year? The simplest analysis suggests that the compensation package is high on retirement benefits in comparison to the private sector, but low in pay. Clearly retirement is high; whether pay is low is not so clear. I shall argue that federal employees are, simultaneously, overpaid and underpaid.

Structural Characteristics. Consider, for example, one of the twenty-four occupations surveyed by the Bureau of Labor Statistics for its annual National Survey of Professional, Administrative, Technical, and Clerical Pay in March 1983—that of Accountant. The BLS set up six levels for accountants, identified the comparable General Services (GS) levels, and found that the average salary for the comparable GS level was below that in the private sector as of March 1983 *for every level* (see table 2).

TABLE 2
PAY OF ACCOUNTANTS

BLS Level	Average Private Salary	GS Level	Average GS Salary
I	$19,519	5	$15,163
II	23,264	7	18,786
III	27,346	9	22,731
IV	34,244	11	27,723
V	41,862	12	33,489
VI	51,798	13	40,319

SOURCE: U.S. Department of Labor, Bureau of Labor Statistics, *National Survey of Professional, Administrative, Technical, and Clerical Pay, March 1983*, September 1983, pp. 10, 77–79.

When we consider, however, the distribution of accountants among the six levels in the public and private sector, the picture changes (see table 3). The federal government has placed far more of its accountants at higher levels; 55.5 percent are at the two highest levels surveyed versus 8.1 percent in the private sector. The average salary for accountants in the federal government, weighted at each level, is $30,863 versus only $28,079 in the private sector. Thus the federal government "underpays" in each category of equivalent work, but overpays its accountants by 9.9 percent in comparison to the private sector. In other words, the federal government could increase pay for accountants to the private

TABLE 3
DISTRIBUTION OF ACCOUNTANTS

Private Sector			Federal Government		
Level	Number	Percent	Level	Number	Percent
I	14,446	13.3	5	432	2.4
II	24,627	22.7	7	1,177	6.4
III	38,498	35.5	9	2,107	11.5
IV	22,037	20.3	11	4,415	24.1
V	7,319	6.8	12	6,467	35.3
VI	1,423	1.3	13	3,702	20.2
Total	108,350			18,300	
Average salary	$28,079			$30,863	

SOURCES: U.S. Department of Labor, Bureau of Labor Statistics, *A National Survey of Professional, Administrative, Technical, and Clerical Pay, March 1983*, September 1983, pp. 10, 77–79; and Office of Personnel Management, "Occupations of Federal White-Collar and Blue-Collar Workers," October 31, 1981.

sector level and *reduce* its wage bill by nearly 10 percent—if its work force were structured in the same manner.

The tendency of the federal government to have relatively more employees at higher grade levels than does the private sector shows up in other occupations as well: 46.4 percent of the government's general attorneys are in the two highest of the six levels for attorneys whereas only 17.6 percent of the private sector attorneys are at these two levels. Although underpayment by the federal government for attorneys is considerable at each level, the weighted average salary is a great deal closer: only 8.4 percent higher in the private sector. Of the 528,328 private sector engineers working for establishments included in the BLS survey, only 11.6 percent were at the three highest of the eight BLS levels versus 44.7 percent of 75,149 federal engineers (all professional engineers). Salaries are lower for each level in the federal sector; the private sector pays 20–30 percent more at several levels, but weighted average pay in the private sector is only 3.4 percent above that in the federal sector. Thus, placing employees in higher grades has, in this case, virtually eliminated underpayment. In 1982, the Office of Management and Budget made comparisons for twenty-one of twenty-three occupations surveyed by BLS in 1981 and found such overgrading in eighteen of them.

Causes of Overgrading. There are possible explanations for this "over-grading": historically, a substitution of promotions for salary increases during years when the executive and congressional branches have held pay increases below those in the private sector; rapid promotion to compensate for low entry-level wages; agency limitations on hiring through personnel ceilings rather than dollars (the "slot" constraint); and agency pressures to overgrade positions.

One study found overgrading—simply an erroneous evaluation of a job—in over 11 percent of federal positions (almost 21 percent of the three highest general schedule levels) and undergrading in 3.3 percent, most of it in grades 1 through 9. Grading errors are only part of the explanation; another part of the explanation may be that the jobs really do merit the grade they have received, either because federal work is more demanding than private work, or because federal agencies have failed to use the division of labor as effectively as have their private counterparts: the work is not efficiently organized to minimize labor costs. One reason for failure to rationalize work management is the limit on federal personnel by agency, the slot limitation, which is reported to be the significant constraint rather than the budget for salaries and expenses.

Is federal work more complex and responsible for, say, engineers or accountants, than private work? Overall one has to doubt this premise, although it may be true for some agencies. It would not surprise me if the Nuclear Regulatory Commission's engineers were distributed in higher grades than engineers in the private sector, but I would question whether the Army Corps of Engineers or the Federal Highway Administration could justify more highly graded engineering staffs than the private sector.

In summary, the federal government actually overpays its work force for at least some occupations because of overgrading and, probably, poor management of workload; at the same time, it underpays (but does not necessarily undercompensate) those who really are doing the work of the grade level they hold.

Recommendations

If the federal work force were structured as is the private work force, the government's wage bill could be 5 to 10 percent less a year than it is—or $3 billion in 1986, rising to $4 billion in 1990, even if it paid private sector wages and salaries. Savings would eventually be achieved in retirement as well.

Solving the complex problem of federal pay and retirement will not be easy. Removing the slot constraint is a possibility, but because agencies have no economic incentive to limit their personnel costs any more than they do the number of people employed, this would be a mistake.

Instead, the Office of Management and Budget should set target grade distributions by agency and occupation, such as engineer, accountant, and so forth. Each agency could then develop a plan to achieve this target by various means at its disposal: attrition, downgrading of positions, and the like. Civil service rules, especially the provision that employees can keep a prior grade and pay for two years if their jobs are downgraded, as well as the difficulty of establishing grade distributions would mean that full savings would take several years to achieve. The benefits, however, would be very great, both to the budget (the taxpayer) and the civil service itself. A grade distribution closer to that in the private sector would reduce the overall wage bill considerably while still allowing pay for each grade closer to the private sector. Far from being a substitute for low pay, the civil service retirement system is additional compensation that is made even more expensive by the overpayment of federal employees. Both should be changed.

Notes

1. 1984 Annual Report of the Board of Trustees of the Federal Old-Age and Survivors Insurance and Disability Insurance Trust Funds (Washington, D.C.: Government Printing Office), p. 73.

2. Robert W. Hartman, *Pay and Pensions for Federal Workers* (Washington, D.C.: Brookings Institution, 1983), p. 2.

The "Safety Net" Programs in the Second Reagan Administration

Kenneth Clarkson

My purpose here is to present a sketch of where the Reagan administration now stands in relation to budget changes in the "safety net" programs, outline some principles underlying budget changes, discuss some changes that the administration should undertake, and expand on some of my own ideas.

Background

Our domestic budget is really a transfer budget. If we examine the most recent available data, we find substantial redistribution. The lowest one-fifth of our population, measured by income, gains approximately $90 billion, while the highest one-fifth loses about $180 billion through redistribution. Interestingly, the highest income quintile does receive $8.3 billion from in-kind transfers. On a per capita basis, if in-kind transfers are evaluated at their market cost, then, individuals in the lowest income quintile increase their effective after-tax income from $317 to $3,463, while those in the highest quintile, who had $16,129, fall to $12,905, as a result of taxes and transfer programs. During the first Reagan administration, many were concerned about those people most affected by the transfer policies. As the most recent data suggest, however, some groups traditionally categorized as poor have improved their economic position in society. Real income of the elderly and female-headed households, for example, rose between 1981 and 1983. These improvements in economic well-being were shared by all income quintiles for the elderly and female-headed households.

Other evidence, however, suggests that everything is not altogether rosy. According to one survey, more people were poor in 1983 than in 1982. Where are these people coming from then?

The big change in poverty comes from the category of young, single people. This suggests that the major problem for the poor reflected general economic conditions rather than the state of federal programs during that time. These statistics are important, because they give us a sense of where we have been and point to where we can go.

Factors in Administration Changes

As for budget changes, several factors will help us understand the direction of the next administration. The first relates to the proper role of government: does a given function or agency compete with the private sector? If so, the administration should present proposals to eliminate that function or agency. When I was in OMB, I made such recommendations, although not all of them were implemented.

In addition, the administration should press for a reduction or elimination of agencies identified as advocacy organizations. Organizations like Vista and Legal Services Corporation, whose roots lie in the Great Society activities and the like are candidates for significant budget reductions, including the possibility of no funding at all.

The second factor is federalism. If the states or localities can manage a certain function better than the federal government, then the administration should recommend that that function be carried out by states, even when it is financed by the federal government.

We should also see more cross-cutting proposals than we have seen in the past: broad budget freezes including general COLA limitations, for example. This type of budget cut has wide appeal because "equal" sacrifice seems fair. The forthcoming budget should also contain a number of recommendations that incorporate management savings techniques, such as those presented in the Grace Commission report.

Major Structural Changes

Major structural changes, however, will account for the most fundamental budget changes. These include changes in incentives for program participants, incentives for program managers, or eligibility requirements for program beneficiaries. In some cases, these structural changes will be directly linked to the political incentives that exist in both the administration and Congress.

FIRST. As an example of a major structural change, let me propose the federal integrated recapture of subsidies tax (FIRST). Under this proposal, all recipients of federal in-kind or income support programs, subsidized loans, or other such programs would receive a T-2 form, like the current W-2 form, providing them and the U.S. Treasury with an accurate report on the value of federal benefits received. Those benefits, then, could be subject to a graduated tax and could be integrated into the existing tax system. FIRST could retain the characteristics of our existing tax system (that is, the poor pay no taxes while the wealthy pay high taxes) and could be adjusted to reflect the nature of the subsidy. For example, in the case of medical care, the insurance value, not the out-of-pocket benefits received by an individual, would be counted as the value of benefits received.

FIRST could be easily integrated with existing accounting systems, automatically taking into consideration such circumstances as the $8 billion worth of in-kind subsidies received by the highest income quintile that are not included in the current tax base.

Changes in AFDC. At this point I will discuss some structural changes including an example of a structural change that did occur and then mention some major safety net programs that could be modified. In 1981, a major structural change representing more than three dozen modifications of program rules and procedures occurred in the Aid to Families with Dependent Children (AFDC) program. The modified program incorporated many new incentives that in their totality encouraged participants to make better choices between work and leisure. In their isolation many of the specific rule changes were difficult to understand. Some of them, such as the elimination of income disregards and gross income eligibility limits, caused a .huge outcry among AFDC supporters.

Contrary to the administration's position, critics claimed that existing AFDC participants, particularly those with some earnings, would fall back on the system, becoming completely dependent on welfare instead of increasing their work force participation. The administration's structural change in the AFDC program evolved from a comprehensive proposal by Robert Carleson who had been welfare director under Governor Reagan in California and was special assistant to the president for policy development in 1981. As welfare director he oversaw numerous changes in the California welfare system and was aware of the various consequences and interactions with other federal and state programs that result from modifying the rules governing the AFDC program. Using this knowledge, he was able to improve the work incentives of program recipients and simultaneously to create budget savings of approximately $2 billion.

This package of reforms passed both the House and the Senate early in the administration, during the "honeymoon." It was accepted virtually in its totality, without major changes either by the Senate or by the House, and all of the cries about the undesirable consequences have proved unfounded. In fact, there has been a strong favorable response by many administrators and participants to the changes in this program.

The structural reforms in the AFDC program freed resources to increase benefits to participants who remained on the program, because some who were previously receiving benefits were no longer eligible. In fact, since the changes were introduced, thirty-eight states have elected to increase their benefit levels. In those states the real income of those remaining in the program has actually risen since the AFDC changes were implemented.

Other Reforms. Still, other desirable structural reforms, such as the mandatory community-work experience requirement, which is currently voluntary in the AFDC program, should be implemented. The data from the states with optional community-work experience programs suggest that this system works quite well, and I expect to see similar proposals in the future.

Budgetary Savings and Program Improvements

Perhaps, then, major structural changes could be made in other programs producing budgetary savings with program improvements. In AFDC and other programs, the next administration should initiate additional structural reforms and management changes that will eliminate or reduce the possibility of eligibility or benefit-level errors. For example, AFDC could be modified to provide assistance to minor mothers only if they live in the same household with their own parents. Studies indicate that providing higher payments to young teenage mothers when they live in separate households has contributed to the breaking up of families. This sort of change in incentives should be proposed in future budgets.

Additional changes to encourage family responsibility through improved child support should also be instituted. In view of continuing problems with the enforcement of child support payments, we should consider modifying the incentive structures to make collections more likely or to lower the cost of using the current child support system, or both.

In other income supplementation areas, such as Supplementary Security Income, where identifying the population is relatively straight-forward with a low probability of error, I do not believe that major changes should be implemented.

In the food stamp program, budget proposals should revise the ways in which states manage their resources. Under the current system, the states are virtually free of liability for their errors in eligibility determination or benefit calculations. In fact, to date no states have paid the penalty for error rates that exceed the current legal levels.

If states do not bear the consequences of making erroneous decisions, we economists predict that they will make more errors. In fact, that pattern seems to hold true in a comparison of programs like food stamps with AFDC in which the effective incentive structures governing error payments are quite different. The administration, then, should introduce changes making the agents, in this case the states, more fiscally responsible for error payments.

The administration should also propose a mandatory community work-experience requirement for the food stamp program similar to that proposed for the AFDC program.

Until more far-ranging proposals are accepted, we should continue to re-recommend such minor management proposals as simplifying calculations and application forms in all benefit programs.

In Medicaid, efforts should be made to introduce improved incentives to all parties involved in the program. These incentives would apply to those who use the Medicaid system, to physicians, and to hospitals. Consider, for example, minor changes to improve user incentives. Although the amounts—$1.00 to $1.50 per visit for physicians, $1.00 to $2.00 per day for hospitals—that have been proposed in the past budget do not sound as if they are enough to alter people's behavior, evidence from other programs where nominal user charges have been introduced indicates that low-income individuals will reduce unnecessary use of medical care under such incentives.

As for the school lunch program, I recommend minor changes. Past proposals such as requiring all school lunch programs to have the same COLA formula and improving verification procedures are desirable changes. Incidentally, in a system in which all benefits are potentially taxable, such as the FIRST system previously described, a verification system would be unnecessary because the parents would automatically get a form stating the benefits for that year, and if they were in a high enough income class, those benefits could be taxed.

Major changes in programs involving provision of supplemental food, such as the Women, Infants, and Children food program and others, are unlikely. Veterans' benefits will also probably not undergo any major changes either, primarily because so much of the veterans' budget is a result of the eligibility system—unless, of course, broadly based COLA changes are accepted.

Potential structural changes in other domestic programs, however, are very desirable. For example, the administration's previous proposal to alter the incentives in foster care and adoption by paying less of the

35

expense for the second and third years that the child is in the foster care or temporary residence, will encourage those agencies to place children in permanent homes more rapidly.

As for training and employment, I do not recommend major changes, except changes with relatively minor budgetary consequences, such as the youth opportunity wage. This structural change has the potential for significantly improving job opportunities and training for youth, with little impact on the budget.

Finally, in education, the administration should attempt to modify access to student aid. In previous budget cycles, the administration attempted to change from a grant-loan-work sequence (that is, grants first, loans next, and work last) to a requirement for students to do some work before receiving grants. The administration's past student aid proposal would increase the total dollar subsidy to low-income students, and I find it difficult to explain why this proposal has not been accepted in previous budgets.

I hope to have communicated my views on future budgetary changes and some of the principles that underlie them.

Discussion

RALPH HALLOW, *Washington Times:* I am concerned about your suggestion, Dr. Anderson, that the civil service pay be increased in order to stop "stuffing" the higher grades. But why would it stop stuffing?

ANNELISE ANDERSON, Hoover Institution: I was not recommending that civil service pay be increased. I recommended that OMB institute slot controls: only so many 11s, 12s, 13s, and 14s could then occupy a given position in a given agency.

How to implement such controls is a very complicated matter. It could be done, however. Federal employees are entitled to two years' saved pay and grade if their jobs are downgraded. At the end of two years, however, we would have a much lower-graded work force in terms of the numbers of people at different levels. The pay could be raised in all areas and still result in a lower federal outlay for personnel costs than we have now.

Nothing stops federal agencies from stuffing the higher grades, because the only limit they have now is a ceiling on the number of employees they can have. They get a salary and expense budget that includes money for equipment and consultants and so forth. If they can hire only one more person but have a little slush fund of money, obviously, they hire a highly qualified person at a high grade rather than one at a lower grade. The system provides incentives to have people at higher grades.

One suggestion about federal pay is to split the general schedule so that the wages of some employees who are recruited and paid locally could be determined in local markets. That makes a lot of sense. Obviously, when 2.8 million people, including the Postal Service and the TVA, are being paid under this system or a related one, it is going to be complicated. There are a lot of details.

LARRY THOMPSON, General Accounting Office: First, with respect to the federal retirement system, I think the data you have presented overstate the case, although I agree with your general conclusion. The federal civil service retirement system lumps together all the retirement, disability, and survivor protection that the federal government offers its employees. The proper comparison, then, has to be with all the retirement, survivor, and disability protection a private sector employer offers. The comparisons you reported tend to omit the costs of private disability insurance, private life insurance, money purchase plans, saving thrift plans, and the like. These considerations narrow the gap but do not eliminate it.

Probably the most egregious feature of the civil service retirement system is full retirement at age fifty-five with thirty years of service. The average civil servant does not retire at age fifty-five; the average is about sixty-one or sixty-two. Our data showed that the average retirement age for the civil service was not much different from that of large private sector employers.

Nonetheless the opportunity is there for full retirement benefits at age fifty-five, and some government employers do take advantage of it. Private sector plans tend to offer retirement at age fifty-five; that's a very common provision. Almost invariably, though, early retirement in the private sector entails some sort of decrement of 3 or 4 percent per year. Perhaps the civil service system should imitate that practice and look at whether the full indexing is really necessary, especially before the worker attains the normal retirement age. We should make it less enticing for people to pack up and leave as soon as they get their thirty years in.

Mr. Levy, I agree with you: the aged are probably better off than popular conception would have it. Of course, our large increases in social security may have something to do with their prosperity.

We must also be sensitive to the income distribution among the aged. There are pockets of real poverty, mainly among singles and mainly among women. Moreover, an unusually large fraction of the aged, while not in poverty, are not much above poverty. Although we may not want to take a whole lot away from them, we certainly have room to consider not giving them a whole lot more.

The real problem in dealing with the issue of public versus private support for the income of the aged is the fact that different aged individuals will find themselves in different positions when it comes to taking advantage of private sector options. If social security were scaled down gradually, perhaps the private pension system would expand appropriately, larger IRA accounts would be approved, and the like. The private sector might, in fact, assume more responsibility for supporting the aged.

The trouble is that we have no reason to believe that such efforts in the private sector will work for, say, the poorest third of the aged population, perhaps even the poorer half. The distribution of pension benefits and the other savings is rather skewed. While this new policy would work, it would work best for those with higher incomes. Therefore, we may have to think about changing the social security structure to make it more redistributive: reducing benefits for the high-wage workers by more than for the low-wage workers, because the private sector benefits will accrue to the high-wage workers. And we may also consider such a restructuring of social security to be fair because, after all, government income security and health programs support the lower-income people with outlays and subsidize the higher-income people with tax expenditures. As the pensions, IRAs, and the like expand, the tax expenditures expand, so the poor will benefit, too.

A more redistributive social security program may be in order then, and academics who worry about the lower rates of return for the high-wage workers than for the lower-wage workers may have to just live with it. The disparity may get worse, if other consistent reforms are instituted.

As for altering the relative roles of social security and means-tested programs, income attempts to shift more of the responsibility to the means-tested programs run up against the problem that a large fraction of the aged are not far above the poverty line. As social security benefits are reduced and Supplemental Security Income benefits increased, very quickly higher and higher numbers of the aged population come under the SSI program. If we are at all concerned about lifetime incentives to save or to work, we certainly do not want very many people on SSI. SSI imposes a 100 percent tax rate against savings and thereby provides absolutely no incentive at all to save over a lifetime, if someone judges himself likely to fall into the means-tested programs.

Finally, I am a bit skeptical about the social security trust fund projections for the 1990s. I cannot believe that Congress will allow $40–50 billion a year to pour into the trust funds above the amount needed to pay benefits. Personally, I have always suspected that a system is better off if it does not have a lot of extra money; otherwise, the temptation is always to increase benefits. I believe that we will have a bigger problem earlier in the twenty-first century than the projections show. Neither do I believe that Congress would cut benefits for a very long time in a budget-balancing mode without sooner or later making offsetting adjustments on the tax side.

An earlier comment reminded me of a little flap about a year and a half ago over expenditure cutbacks in the airport trust fund. Some argued that we might as well cut the ticket tax now, because there is no point in letting all that money come in if we weren't going to spend it. We must be careful when we try to close the budget deficit by cutting expenditures in trust fund accounts, while looking only at the way these changes affect the unified budget. In making certain kinds of cuts, we create a structure that does not make sense in the context of the trust fund itself, and in that case, the changes eventually get undone. We cannot go a long way toward closing the current budget deficit by constraining social security benefits because sooner or later we will end up restructuring the revenue side as well. One could argue that some trimming of the cost-of-living adjustment would make good sense from the standpoint of the unified budget, and, for the next few years, it also makes good sense from the standpoint of the trust fund. Although the projections of the trust fund balance are positive right now, they show that the financial condition remains a little risky between now and 1989 or so, and another recession could cause us to have another round of hand wringing over how to finance social security.

DR. ANDERSON: Given the current situation in social security, I would be perfectly happy to look at a long-term reduction in the richness of the benefit structure (not benefit reductions in terms of checks in the mail). Making it more redistributive would actually be taken care of by taxing benefits on which people have not yet paid taxes, which is the employer's contribution, and means testing that aspect of it. As the trust fund builds up, as it will, and if we succeed in reducing the benefit structure during the twenty-first century (that is, the benefits for the people who are now paying taxes), I think reducing social security taxes is a great idea. I would be for it.

MICKEY LEVY, Fidelity Bank, Philadelphia: Larry, I concur with you that a large portion of social security beneficiaries are poor or near-poor. But if you say the program is well structured for 50 percent of the beneficiaries, but not well structured for the other 50 percent, then you are talking about a $170-billion-a-year program with room for improvement.

If we restructured the program, we could save money, but we could also be more generous to the truly needy elderly and the near-poor. I think taxing benefits that exceed contributions would go a long way. That does increase income taxes. I would be willing to use a portion of that amount, a sizable portion, to redistribute to the poor recipients. I would also like to use the residual portion, however, to reduce social security tax rates.

We now have a program that is not particularly well structured for what it was intended to do, and it is a very expensive program, with a lot of room for reform.

JACK MEYER, American Enterprise Institute: I would go even a bit farther than Dr. Anderson on the issue of pay for the civil service. The government's survey of pay comparability is very badly flawed in the respect she mentioned as well as in some others. A number of categories are left out of the groups with which federal workers are compared. This makes me quite suspicious about what the "control group" would look like if the survey were done in a more representative way. For example, small firms are not included in the sample; they tend to have slower wage growth. State and local workers are not included. I think they also have had slower wage growth, but that may turn around from time to time. Moreover, many jobs are left out. Not only is each job category "stuffed," as Dr. Anderson has pointed out, but also only one-fourth of all federal jobs are accounted for by employment in the government's survey of private sector jobs. Of the ones not covered, there are more jobs with slower pay growth.

Federal workers are being compared with a very biased base, with a disproportionate share of high-growth jobs. When we compare federal workers with that base, then they always appear to be falling behind, unless they get whopping pay increases. I can recall measuring the pay of federal workers against that of state workers and finding that a GS-13 or 14 made more than the attorneys general of many states, and even the governors of a few. Something has got to be a little askew here.

STEWART GODDIN, Department of the Treasury: To the discussion of the two pay schedules, I would like to mention geographic adjustment and functional adjustment. The OPM tables do not take into account geographic adjustment (cost-of-living differences in various parts of the country); they probably should. Perhaps the federal government should have cost-of-living adjustments depending on the location of the job. It can be a real problem to entice a federal employee to leave a low-cost area and return to Washington. Knowing that it will cost him $10,000 a year more to live in Washington, he insists on a bigger promotion. When the time comes to send him back, it's hard to demote him. I suggest, then, some geographic differential.

As for the functional adjustment, I don't know how much work has been done on that. Some federal government functions (for example, policy analysis) may require more higher-grade people than is necessary on average for the private sector as a whole; other functions may require a lower overall grade average. That question probably should be explored more.

On another matter, I am not very confident that OMB or OPM understands the work levels in various agencies well enough to allocate grade slots. I agree that the present system where an agency is given a number of slots and it doesn't make any difference whether they are filled with GS-15's or GS-2's is absolutely crazy. It might be better to give agencies or individual managers more flexibility by giving them an overall personnel budget ceiling in dollars (perhaps combined with a maximum number of slots) and leaving it up to the agency or manager to determine the optimum combination of grades.

BYRON FIELDING, *Housing Affairs Letter:* There are whole areas here that nobody has mentioned—housing, community development, public works, or infrastructure. What savings could be realized in those areas, or have they been cut so drastically that there is nothing left to save?

DR. ANDERSON: On the subject of subsidized housing, whether it is the public housing program or the Section 8 subsidized housing programs, a voucher system is a more effective market mechanism than a payment to the landlord of the difference between what the tenant pays and the rent charged, because it encourages the tenant to shop to get the most for his money.

The groups interested in these programs want to increase constantly the absolute number and the percentage of the population receiving subsidized housing for the poor. This program is not an entitlement. Although they would like it to become an entitlement, we just cannot afford to make it an entitlement.

I believe that subsidized housing ought to be abolished. We should go toward cash assistance for the poor, and certainly not try to build housing, because the federal government does it very badly. We really ought not to subsidize housing as a separate item at all. We should freeze these programs and gradually eliminate them, and whatever is physically owned by the government should ultimately be turned over to the private sector. I would not have subsidized housing programs as part of an overall welfare package.

MR. FIELDING: Not even vouchers, as the Heritage Foundation suggested?

DR. ANDERSON: I would have the vouchers as an interim way for the people now in the program. I would switch from the current program to vouchers; we already have some vouchers in the system. I would look at phasing out that program eventually, however. It is still increasing every year because of prior commitments, for example, to build public housing, so there are more and more units coming on line, for more and more people. I think the total number of people is 11 or 12 million, and the number of units is around 4 million. That's much higher than it was when the Reagan administration took office.

Another alternative is to look at a program that does not permanently establish a subsidized housing unit, whether it is a vouchered unit or whether it is a physical unit, but meets a temporary need. We need the leeway to say, "You know, we've got a lot of people in trouble this year, and we're going to give so many vouchers." The vouchers, which would stay with individual people, would expire when the people went off subsidized housing. This system then reduces the number of people on the program and gives Congress the flexibility in future years to request more or less without making permanent the number of subsidized housing units in the system.

JOHN WEICHER, American Enterprise Institute: We could get rid of the Urban Development Action Grant Program and save some small change. That program provides subsidies to private firms at the discretion of the local government, while other private firms are doing the same things without discretionary subsidies. The rationale for the program seems to be that it redirects activities from suburbs to cities to a minor extent, at a fairly significant cost.

PETER TROPP, Housing and Urban Development: Without belittling what we have been able to accomplish in accordance with those principles on which President Reagan was elected, in many cases we have run up against the congressional talent for devising a new form of construction program to block such eminently sensible management changes as vacancy rules. We face, for instance, the preposterous notion that we should fully subsidize a vacant public housing unit indefinitely, and so forth.

Without going through a long litany of what we have not succeeded in doing so far, how could we be more effective in selling some of the solutions or goals, or implementing them, given the congressional propensity to hook housing bills to IMF bills, block rules changes from going through, and the like?

DR. ANDERSON: I have two suggestions: a balanced budget tax limitation amendment and a line-item veto for the president in the Constitution.

The power of the special interest groups and of the congressional committee structure is now strong enough to block a great deal. I recommend these policies because I think they are right, not because I think that the Congress is going to vote for them. Short-term considerations are often at stake. User fees seem to be a very reasonable idea. The only user fees the Reagan administration could institute were accompanied by sharply higher program levels. That was true for the Federal Aviation Administration with the ticket tax; it was true of the gasoline tax; it was also true for the Patent Office, where we got 100 percent collections but where we also hired a lot more people to expedite

43

processing. The political equation is, "I'll pay, provided you give me more. But if I'm already getting it, I'm not going to start paying for it."

This attitude poses a real problem that we citizens must face. We can always balance the budget by raising taxes. A 40 percent increase in corporate and individual income taxes will balance the budget. Think of the tax you paid last April and add 40 percent: imagine everyone's doing that, including corporations. That would be an enormous hit and economically undesirable for long-term growth.

Do we want to do that? Do we want to raise taxes, or do we want to eliminate some government programs?

MR. TROPP: By passing the balanced budget amendment or the line-term veto, which are obviously fairly long-term propositions, you are essentially throwing in the towel. . . .

DR. ANDERSON: The date of effective implementation would make them long-term propositions. If, however, a few more state governments passed a call for a constitutional convention to examine the question of an amendment to balance the budget, Congress would act immediately because Congress would not allow a constitutional convention to be called. The Senate has already passed a version of a balanced budget tax limitation amendment; the bill passed the House, but not by the two-thirds that was needed. The effect on the budget process would be quite swift. We don't have to wait until the balanced budget amendment is passed and implemented for it to start having an effect.

KENNETH CLARKSON, Law and Economics Center: I strongly support the balanced budget tax limitation amendment and also want to highlight the use of reconciliation for restraining governmental growth. In the reconciliation process all budget choices are considered simultaneously as opposed to separately, resulting in a very powerful mechanism for assessing budget priorities and making trade-offs. I think that that process was largely responsible for the major gains made by the administration in 1981.

Short of instituting balanced-budget and related changes, a comprehensive reconciliation bill that includes all budget proposals would produce more desirable outcomes.

RONALD HOFFMAN, Department of the Treasury: I am interested in several points that Jack Meyer touched on about Medicare. First, although the notion of taking care of catastrophic illness is attractive, I am concerned with the presumption that there be no limit on the amount of aid given to the recipient. The impact of that on future budgets gives me pause.

Perhaps we need to begin to discuss such limits explicitly. That is a difficult subject to talk about, but I think it is necessary.

Second, to what extent, apart from the obvious political attractiveness, should age be a reason to subsidize health care?

Certainly, discussion of plans that base coverage of catastrophic illness on the income of the recipient moves away from consideration of a non-means-tested subsidy. The escalation of medical care costs and expenditures adds pressure to relate subsidies negatively to income and wealth and to make the relationship increasingly more stringent. Thus, depending on the system adopted, some elderly may receive zero subsidy; that is, their subsidy would be phased out. Then income rather than age is the criterion.

DR. MEYER: I will address both issues. In answer to your first question, there is a concern that a full stop-loss provision or catastrophic illness provision in a program like Medicare—or indeed, in any insurance— becomes a license to perform almost any procedure, to keep plugs in indefinitely, or, indeed, to do all kinds of heroic and radical techniques that might not otherwise be done. The solution, however, is not to keep the current benefit design, but to change it to one with coverage for catastrophic problems, and rely on the movement toward a prospective payment system in Medicare to avert excessive medical interventions.

If you had asked me this question two years ago before Medicare began to "change its ways," I would have been very worried about this problem. At that time we had a system that paid for whatever people spent in a hospital, with only a few limits.

Now, the Medicare system imposes a set fee for a particular type of illness, such as myocardial infarction, or a particular type of procedure like coronary bypass. In that kind of environment, even if the benefit structure is changed as I suggest, hospitals that are very profligate in "Star Wars" technology or "Star Wars" experimentation on patients will lose money.

You raise a legitimate problem, but I prefer to get at it through a prospective payment system, rather than relying on cost-sharing at the "back end," as we have been doing. I would feel comfortable changing that cost sharing as long as we have prospective payment, assuming that we can make the new system work.

Now, with regard to the other, even more interesting question of whether age is a sufficient criterion for subsidized health care, I could accept a situation in which need gradually replaced age as the primary criterion for how we distribute money in health care and, indeed, in other social services. Over time, age has not been a bad proxy for need, to some extent. Clearly, elderly people spend more money on health than nonelderly people, but we know that we have subgroups of the elderly that are not only very healthy, but very wealthy. In some sense everyone has paid into programs like Medicare through their working years. Increasingly, however, we realize that we cannot afford to subsidize everybody to the same extent and still meet other national objectives. The ultimate end of graduated subsidies, which I favor, is that a person could be wealthy enough to handle all but the most catastrophic expenses. I could live with such a system, particularly if I thought that low-income people who are now turned away from an emergency room or a hospital bed might get in.

DIANE REIS, Capital Publications: Dr. Clarkson, what do you think the outlook is for some of the antipoverty programs that were not mentioned, such as Community Services Block Grant, Low-Income Energy Aid, and Head Start? I'd also like to address that question to Dr. Anderson, as a former OMB official.

DR. CLARKSON: Throughout the first administration, the policy has been to encourage the use of block grants whenever possible for federal antipoverty programs. I anticipate that this policy will continue in the next four years. Because block grants provide funds to states in an unconstrained form, they coincide with the president's goal of increasing federalism. With respect to block grant budgetary changes, I expect some changes to reflect inflation but not necessarily full price indexation.

Low-Income Energy Assistance, however, is a slightly different type of transfer program that has become less and less what it was originally intended to be—assistance to offset a sudden increase in energy prices. The administration has struggled with this particular program during the past two or three years, and I have less complete forecasts for it. In the near future I expect the program will maintain its status quo, but attempts should continue to retarget expenditures to the states with excessively cold winters.

MS. REIS: Even though President Reagan's budget has recommended phasing out the Community Services Block Grant completely, do you think it will still survive?

DR. CLARKSON: Many of the funded activities in the Community Services Block Grant (CSBG) can be traced to Great Society programs. The administration has proposed that these activities be funded by the administration's Social Services Block Grant. CSBG is also not a pure block grant in that Congress specifies how the money should be spent on various activities rather than letting the states decide on the allocation of funds. Consequently, I expect that CSBG will be treated differently from other block grants. I would add the footnote that federal programs that provide funds for advocacy groups have been targeted for significantly high budget cuts, including zero funding.

Any of the block grants put together by the Reagan administration as a way of combining a large number of discretionary programs and giving the states or localities the authority to determine spending allocations, though, will and should be relatively protected. If they fall into the congressional-directed spending or advocacy categories, however, I would say just the opposite.

DR. ANDERSON: Community Development Block Grant and general revenue sharing are products of previous Republican administrations. The Community Development Block Grant was modified by this administration and made less categorical. As I remember, it was during the Nixon administration that a group of programs were combined to create CDBG, just as we combined a lot in this administration. Cutting out what you have blocked up is rather a problem.

Nevertheless, funds in general revenue sharing, which is a Nixon program, and the Community Development Block Grant are distributed according to needs formulas to different levels of government. Community Development Block Grant is virtually a general revenue-sharing program, in terms of how the funds are distributed.

Of course, one argument against these programs is this: what are we doing? The federal government does not have any revenue to share.

WAYNE VROMAN, The Urban Institute: I will premise my comments on two assumptions. One is that we will have a deficit for quite a while, and, two, the government transfers will continue to be a major portion of overall federal expenditures.

Given those assumptions, I see three general areas where transfers could be cut or their rate of growth slowed through the rest of this decade and later.

Probably we have a general consensus in this society that we should not pay government transfers to people who are working most of the year. With that in mind, I have tabulated the Current Population Survey, which identifies twelve individual major transfer payment programs and asks the individual how many weeks he or she worked last year. When people in the survey are cross-classified, three programs emerge with large numbers of people who work forty or more weeks and also collect a transfer payment. The three programs are unemployment insurance, workers' compensation, and military retirement.

Now unemployment insurance and workers' compensation are special creatures, because many people who collect those benefits do so for a short time until their period of unemployment or temporary disability ends and they go back to work. Military retirement is different. Those people, some of whom are forty to forty-five years old, much below normal retirement age, collect a transfer payment for the entire year and work for the entire year.

Taking away that transfer payment is obviously changing the rules of the game, and people have acquired rights of eligibility for those transfers through prior military service. This transfer payment goes to people with very high incomes, and the dollar amount of the program is large. Many in the program are firmly attached to the labor force and have very low poverty rates. This area might be considered in a general strategy of where to cut transfer payments.

In addition, cuts might be considered for people collecting multiple benefits. Federal civilian workers come to mind here, state and local workers to a much lesser extent.

In contrast to military retirees, though, most people who collect federal civilian pensions do not work at the same time. A number of people aged fifty-five to fifty-nine or sixty to sixty-four, who have exited completely from the labor force are collecting federal civilian pensions. If we are trying to limit the growth in transfer payments, we could treat all transfer payments (including OASDHI) like ordinary income and increase the recapture of those multiple benefits through the tax system. Alternatively, explicit offsets among transfers when there are multiple transfers could also be considered.

Next and probably most important is early retirement, which affects social security as well as private pensions and other retirement programs. In our society men are leaving the labor force at very young ages. According to Labor Department surveys, in the past couple of years about one-sixth of men ages fifty-five to fifty-nine have not worked one day in the entire previous year. The work experience survey also asked, Did you work last year? If the answer was no, the survey further probed and asked, Why didn't you work? Most of those people gave one of two reasons: they had retired, or they were disabled. Making the distinction between being retired and being disabled for those aged fifty-five to fifty-nine is an art form that I am not comfortable with. Most people here at the table would probably say that "disabled" means retired in many cases.

Someone commented earlier that overretirement was a problem with government workers. Many of the retirements in the past ten years in the United States, however, have been initiated by the private sector. Early retirement is one of the private sector adjustments that becomes increasingly prevalent when the economy goes into recession; firms simply flush out older workers, giving them a bridge payment and saying adios. This practice allows firms to retain younger workers, whose annual earnings are a fraction of what more senior workers are making. Even by paying a generous pension, bridge payment, then, the net cost to the firm is not as high as the pension payment alone might suggest.

Until we do something to change expectations about working to age sixty-two, or even higher in an increasingly healthy society, the biggest block of transfer programs will continue to grow, namely, those targeted on the retired.

As for social security, measurable gains can likely be accomplished through inaction. The social security amendments of last year, for example, for the first time started to tax a fraction of social security benefits on incomes over a certain threshold. By inaction, by not changing those thresholds over time, an increasing share of the income of the elderly population will fall above the threshold. Even if half of social security benefits are then taxable, the tax rates on the aged will be effectively raised through this inaction.

Second, I want to argue for retention of the retirement test. In a social security program not in the best financial shape, providing a windfall gain to a whole lot of older people who are eligible for social security but who are still firmly attached to the labor force is foolish. To provide such a windfall benefit to those people on the thin-reeded hope that other people are going to work more later on is to trade a certain drain on the social security trust funds against an improbable wish. Why do we expect to get increased labor supply out of older people when the historical evidence suggests that few older people eligible to go back to work and increase their earnings substantially do in fact go back to work?

Right now, according to the retirement test, if we measure an older person's earnings at the average hourly earnings rate, that person can work about 800 hours per year. If we really want to encourage older people to work more, we can raise the limit of the retirement test, $6,960 this year, up to something like $10,000. We can allow those people more potential hours of work but still prevent the very high-income aged—the people who are eligible and do not collect social security benefits with poverty rates that are essentially zero—from collecting benefits. My research supports these fairly strong assertions. If we really want the social security system to recover financially, then by not raising the income limits above which income starts to be taxed, not raising social security benefits, and by retaining the retirement test in its current form, we are providing a benefit that grows through time, at least in the case of the income taxing, without having to do anything active to change the current social security program.

DR. LEVY: With regard to the retirement test, I would not argue. That is a minor point that I was making. Under the 1983 amendments, the test was watered down, and I go along with that.

As for early retirement, I wholeheartedly agree with you: the trend toward early retirement has been startling, and it has continued. I think the social security system should be neutral on when people retire, rather than discouraging work, as it does now.

Finally, the median age of the working age population is rising, and we have a number of years to change the current benefit structure, not only the OASI benefit structure, but disability, and the way it affects early retirement. We had better have structural reforms fully implemented by the time the postwar baby boom children get into their mid-fifties.

DR. MEYER: I generally agree with the points just made, but I am somewhat troubled with these notions unless we add some qualification to the first two premises. First, on the criterion of working most of the year, I think you would agree with me that there is a class of low-wage workers whom we would not want to rule out of eligibility for government benefits. Indeed, someone earning $3.35 an hour, the minimum wage, gets $6,700 a year; that's more than $3,000 below the poverty line. At the same time, someone not working may be very well off for reasons unrelated to work.

Second, on the criterion of multiple benefits, I also worry about the excessive provision of benefits, such as a case of "five-program" beneficiaries. Many people, however, who simply combine AFDC and food stamps, or some comparable two-program combination are very needy. At the same time, somebody may have one and only one subsidy, but not need it at all.

With those qualifications, I would support your point.

MR. VROMAN: Would you throw social security and these other programs into the tax system, all of them?

DR. MEYER: Yes, if we adopt Dr. Clarkson's proposal, that would all be taken care of through the tax system, and I have no problem with this approach.

DR. ANDERSON: Dr. Levy, would you comment further on the unfairness to women involved in the social security spousal benefit? I like the idea of earnings sharing very much; however, people have claimed that earnings sharing is so expensive that we cannot afford it. Is there a way that we can institute such a system to cut women loose, so they have their benefits established in their own right, whether they earn them as wives, getting credit for half their husbands' earnings, or directly in the labor force?

DR. LEVY: To add to what you said, I find it quite ironic and hypocritical that the government and elected officials urge private sector employers to provide fair, competitive, or even comparable wages to women; yet these same government officials are not aware that the government itself is discriminating against women in their total social security compensation. I am not an expert on earnings-sharing systems although I have read various proposals on this complex issue. There are ways to set up an earnings-sharing system whereby household earnings are split in half, so that when there are divorces, family split-ups, or other circumstances, working or nonworking spouses create and take with them an earnings base that can be used for their own principal insurance amount when they reach retirement. One could be implemented in a way that is not costly but that would require changing the basic social security benefit structure. In my mind, it would be well worth the effort.

DR. CLARKSON: Social security is a topic that we have not spent a lot of time on during the discussion. Perhaps we share the general feeling that social security will not change very much in this administration. This inaction results more from political constraints than from satisfaction with the current social security system. Furthermore, unless social security reforms become popular and contribute to a large number of expected votes, ignoring them might be a very good strategy for this administration or for any political party, as long as the trust funds are sufficient to avoid an immediate crisis—not good public policy, but good politics. We may not act, then, until we get into another crisis.

I have worked a lot with younger people at universities, and most of them tell me they do not expect to get a dime out of social security. As that sector of the population becomes a larger percentage of voters, I think we will feel pressure to reduce the importance of social security for retirement income. At that time, social security will become a smaller and smaller proportion of the federal budget. Ultimately, I suspect, the budget constraints will mandate that all social security payments be counted as taxable income, that some kind of means test will be considered, or both. If this occurs, the social security program will become very different from how it had originally been envisioned.

It is also likely that Medicare will follow a similar legislative path, although we will have to make some important decisions on that program much earlier than we will on the retirement program. This scenario seems as likely as some of the others we have been talking about.

MR. WEICHER: I thank you all for coming. I would like to thank our panel, too.

Selected AEI Publications

AEI Associates Program

21